FOREST MAMMALS

created by
BOBBIE KALMAN

art by
GLEN LOATES

BOBBIE KALMAN / GLEN LOATES

Forest Mammals

The North American Wildlife Series

CRABTREE PUBLISHING COMPANY

The Glen Loates North American Wildlife Series:
Created by Bobbie Kalman
Art by Glen Loates

Editor-in-Chief:
Bobbie Kalman

Researchers:
Moira Daly
Virginia Neale

Writing team:
Bobbie Kalman
Virginia Neale
Moira Daly
Janine Schaub
Christine Arthurs

Editors:

Janine Schaub   Moira Daly
Tilly Crawley   Louise Petrinec
Anne Champagne   Judith Ellis
Christine Arthurs

Illustrations:
Copyright © 1987 MGL Fine Art Limited.

Photographs:
Page 12: Animals Animals/C.C. Lockwood

Design:
Leslie Smart & Associates Limited
Stephen Latimer

Computer layout:
Christine Arthurs

Mechanicals:
Halina Below-Spada   Gerry Lagendyk

Printer:
Bryant Press, with special thanks to Arnie Krause

For Edith, my mother-in-law, on her 95th birthday

Cataloguing in Publication Data

Kalman, Bobbie, 1947-
            Forest Mammals

(The Glen Loates North American wildlife series)
Includes index.
ISBN 0-86505-165-8 (bound) ISBN 0-86505-185-2
(pbk.)

1. Mammals -North America - Juvenile literature. 2.
Forest ecology - Juvenile literature. I. Loates, Glen.
II. Title. III. Series: Kalman, Bobbie, 1947-
The Glen Loates North American wildlife series.

QL715.K34 1987 j599.097

350 Fifth Avenue   120 Carlton Street
Suite 3308   Suite 309
New York   Toronto, Ontario
N.Y. 10118   Canada M5A 4K2

Contents

M. G. LOATES

Forest mammals

A large area of land covered by trees is known as a forest. Sometimes dark and mysterious, sometimes a kaleidoscope of bright colors, the forest is home to many kinds of creatures. The white-tailed deer and the black bear; the chipmunk and the porcupine—these are just a few of the animals that are part of this rich environment. The forest provides these animals and many others with food, water, shelter, and places to hide. It protects them from the hot rays of the sun and the cold chill of the wind.

Many of the animals that live in a forest are mammals. Mammals come in all shapes, sizes, and colors. Some fly, while others climb trees. Some run on the ground; some burrow beneath the earth. Mammals have paws, hoofs, flippers, and even wings. They live in both cold and warm climates. They live in many kinds of forests.

Mammals are the most highly developed animals in the world. Human beings are also mammals. The more you learn about mammals, the more you will appreciate how important they are to us. Read on and find out how mammals live and how they make the forest their home.

Forests are not just trees!

There are several types of forests in North America. Each type provides a variety of animals with food and shelter. The place in which animals feed and live is called their **habitat**.

Some animals prefer a specific type of forest as their habitat, while others can live in almost any kind of woodland. The red squirrel, for example, eats cones, nuts, and seeds. It finds these foods in the **coniferous** forests of the north. Coniferous trees grow cones and do not lose their leaves or needles.

The leaves of **deciduous** trees are broad, change color, and fall in the autumn. Deciduous forests are located in areas where there are at least six months of mild weather each year. In these forests the weather is neither too hot nor too cold. The gray squirrel and deer mouse prefer living in deciduous forests.

In addition to the deciduous and coniferous forests there are large **mixed** forests containing both coniferous and deciduous trees. Many mammals find mixed forests the best source of both plant and animal food.

The forest ecosystem

Each type of forest is made up of living and non-living parts. The trees, plants, insects, and animals are all part of the **living community**. The non-living parts include the soil, water, wind, and energy from the sun. The climate, gases in the air, rocks, rivers, and the shape of the land are also part of this non-living or **physical environment**. The creatures that belong to the living community depend both on one another and on the physical environment. Together, the living community and the physical environment of an area make up an **ecosystem**. The earth is one big ecosystem. The forest is a small one.

Nature's energy flow

All living things in the forest need energy. They need energy to move and grow, eat, breathe, and sleep. Whenever an animal eats a plant, it takes in **food energy**. When an earthworm nibbles on a leaf or a moose chews on a tree bud, energy is passed from plant life to the creature eating the plant.

Energy from the sun

If people and animals eat plants as food, what do plants eat? Plants need food energy to grow healthy and strong, just as animals do. Green plants get energy from the sun. They use this energy to turn water, air, and the nutrients in the soil into starches and sugars. The starches and sugars then store this energy. Plants are called **producers** because they make food energy. People, animals, and insects are **consumers** because they eat the plants that produce energy. When animals or humans eat these plants, they are really getting some of the sun's energy!

You are what you eat

Each creature has its own special diet depending on what kind of energy it needs. Some eat plants, some eat animals, and some eat both in order to stay alive. Animals that eat only plants, such as rabbits and porcupines, are called **herbivores**. The wolf and the lynx are examples of **carnivores**, or meat eaters. Raccoons and other animals that eat plants as well as meat are called **omnivores**. What type of food consumer are you?

Food chains and webs

Every time an animal eats, it takes in food energy. When a berry is eaten by a chipmunk and the chipmunk is eaten by a lynx, energy is passed along a **food chain**. The berry, the chipmunk, and the lynx are each links in one chain. Similarly, the acorn, the mouse, and the wolf are links in another chain. Most food chains are connected to other food chains in the forest. A lynx and a wolf are part of separate food chains, but because they both eat chipmunks and mice, their chains are connected. Connected food chains form a **food web**. Many food webs can be found in one forest.

Decomposers are also a part of all food chains. Decomposers are creatures such as beetles and earthworms. They help break down dead plants and animals into nutrients that are then returned to the environment. Nothing is wasted in nature!

Why are predators important?

Carnivores are also known as **predators**. Because predators kill for their food, many people are afraid of them and often kill them on sight. Yet these predators are only hunting for their natural food as part of the forest food chain.

Predators play an important role in their ecosystems. For example, if people kill too many foxes, the deer mouse population will rise. When there are too many mice, these creatures start eating the food of other animals and that of people. In the end if we upset the balance of nature, we are the ones who will be the losers!

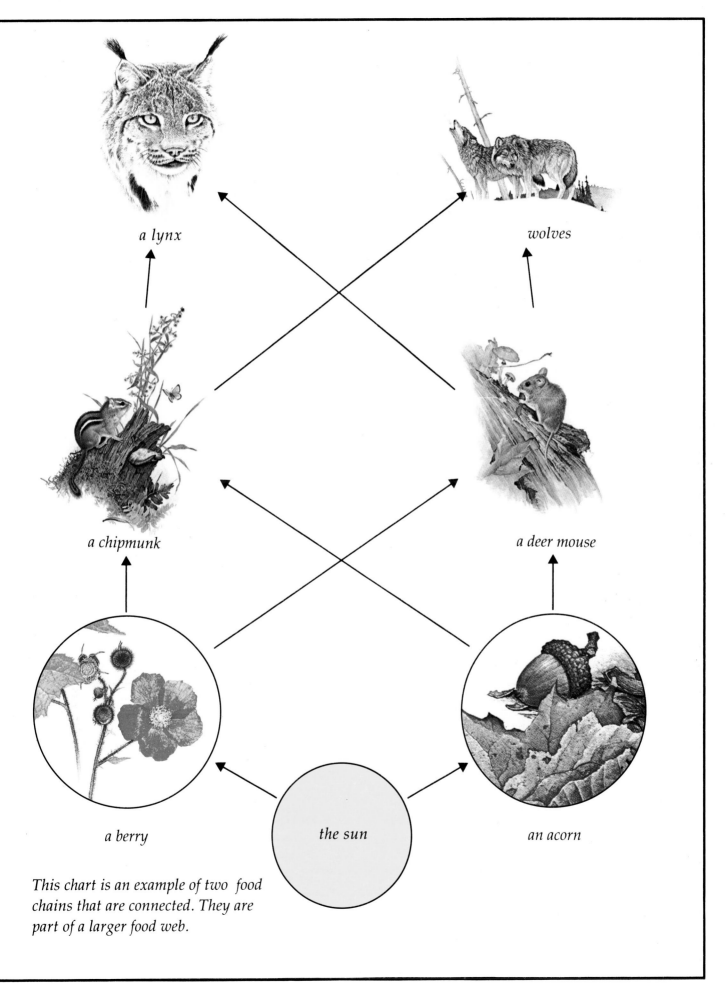

a lynx

wolves

a chipmunk

a deer mouse

a berry

the sun

an acorn

This chart is an example of two food chains that are connected. They are part of a larger food web.

What makes mammals unique?

Only mammal mothers are able to nurse their young.

ammals share some characteristics with other living creatures, but one feature makes them unique. All mammal mothers produce milk to feed their babies. Milk is made in the **mammary glands**. The words "mammal" and "mammary" both come from the same ancient word, *mamma*, which means breast. No other living creatures are able to produce milk.

How are mammals born?

Mammals grow inside their mothers' bodies and most are fully developed when they are born. Other kinds of animals, such as birds and snakes, lay eggs from which their babies later hatch.

Highly developed

Another common feature of mammals is that they are all hairy. Some have a full coat of fur, while others may only have a few hairs! Mammals are more highly developed than other creatures. They have backbones, and they breathe with lungs. Their brains are much bigger than those of other animals.

Warm-blooded

Unlike reptiles, mammals have warm blood. This means that they have a constant, warm body temperature no matter what the weather is like outside. Warm-blooded creatures can live in hot or cold climates and can adapt to changes in the seasons.

The moose

Splash! Splash! Crash! This is the sound of a frightened moose running through water and into the underbrush. If you saw this gigantic animal running towards you, you might be frightened, too. After all, the moose is the biggest deer in the world. It is taller than the largest saddle horse! It has humped shoulders, a short neck, a big heavy head, and a long, drooping snout. The flap of skin hanging from its throat is called a **bell**, or **dewlap**.

Antler antics

Male moose, or **bulls**, start growing antlers in April. For the first few months a covering of skin and hair, called **velvet**, coats the antlers. The velvet is a source of nourishment for the bone while it is growing. When the antlers are fully grown, moose shed their velvet by rubbing it off on tree trunks and shrubs.

The bulls use their full-grown antlers for the first time during the fall **rut**, or mating season. The males run at each other head-on and crash these huge structures together. They are competing for the attention of the females, or **cows**. Once the competition is over, however, it seems the bulls have no further use for their bony headpieces. The antlers fall off and are replaced by a new set the following spring.

Food fit for a moose

Moose are strong swimmers and are at home in the water. Their favorite food is water lilies because these plants supply them with the salt they need in their diets. Moose live in mixed forests that are near rivers and lakes. They often wade into a nearby lake, plunge their heads under the water, and come up with a mouthful of water lily stems and roots. Forest lakes that have a good supply of salty water lilies are often called "moose licks!" Moose also eat a variety of leaves and grasses. In the wintertime they feed on twigs and bark. In fact, the word "moose" comes from the Algonquin Indian word *musée,* meaning "wood-eater" or "bark-stripper."

The massive antlers of a moose are like no other antlers. They look like tree branches and can be more than a meter wide. Some sections between the branches are filled in, creating a wide, ridged surface that looks something like a ribcage.

The marten

Don't ever invite a marten to a party, for it will not come. Martens are not social animals. In fact, they are the most independent animals in the forest. The only reason a marten seeks out other animals is to eat them!

The chuckling season

Even though the marten prefers being alone, it searches for another marten during mating season. Early in June the male leaves his scent on tree trunks, fallen logs, and rocks throughout the forest. When the female picks up a male's scent, she begins to make chuckling noises. A chuckling female soon attracts a mate.

Nature's skydiver

With its slender body, curved claws, and long bushy tail, the marten is ideally suited for tree climbing. Using its tail as a balancing rod, it leaps from branch to branch gracefully and effortlessly. The marten sometimes makes a game of climbing a pine tree and "skydiving" out of it from a height of several meters.

Tunneling around

The marten is an efficient predator. It preys on small animals such as mice, squirrels, voles, hares, and birds, but will also eat insects, fruit, and nuts. Sometimes this mammal tunnels long distances under the snow to look for food or climbs high up in a tree to chase its prey. When the hunting is good, it gathers more food than it needs and hides the extra food in a hollow tree.

The raccoon

There is a forest mammal that you might see visiting your home from time to time. It might unhook the latch on your gate, waddle up to your garbage can, and pull off the lid to see what is inside.

The intruder is about the size of a huge cat and has a bushy tail with four to six dark rings around it. Across its small, pointed face runs a stripe of black fur that looks like a mask, but you would recognize this face anywhere! It is the familiar face of the mischievous raccoon.

The raccoon's agile paws allow it to get into all sorts of mischief. Its forepaws resemble tiny hands with five slender "fingers" tipped with curved claws. A raccoon can use these paws to open clams, pick berries, catch fish and frogs, peel corn, or even pick locks!

Scrounging for food

Raccoons are **nocturnal** animals. They doze away the day in trees, lying flat on their backs or rolled up in balls. They often cover their eyes with their front paws! At night they climb down from their sleeping spots and search for food.

The raccoon is most at home near fresh water. It finds its favorite foods, such as frogs, crayfish, insects, turtles, mice, birds' eggs, and berries, at the shores of ponds or rivers. A raccoon eats almost anything it can scrounge up, plant or animal.

While raccoons usually live in all types of forests, they also settle wherever there are a few trees. You might meet a raccoon in a city park or in a neighborhood ravine.

Baby raccoons

A mother raccoon makes her **den** in any sheltered spot, such as a hollow tree, under some tree roots, or even in a granary or hayloft. She usually has a litter of four babies. The babies venture out into the world when they are about eight weeks old. By the time they are three months old, they are eagerly following their mother around, learning how to catch their own food.

The white-tailed deer

When a white-tailed deer is feeding and moving slowly about, its tail is lowered so that only the outer, reddish brown part shows. Why should this animal be so careful of the position of its tail? The reason is that the white underside of this deer's tail is used to warn other deer that there is danger nearby. A flick of the tail into its upright position is all that is needed to send the deer's companions off into the forest for cover.

Bony branches

The male deer, or **buck**, begins to grow antlers when he is about two years old. The size of the antlers and the number of branches, or **points**, they have depend on how good the deer's diet has been. The antlers of a five-year-old buck are the most highly developed. Before and after this bucks have smaller antlers with fewer points. Antlers grow from May to August. They are shed for the winter.

You might think that these sharp, bony antlers are used for protection. In actual fact, they are not much of a defense at all. Antlers can become entangled in the antlers of other deer or in nearby trees. The deer can then be easily attacked by a predator. The main reason deer use their antlers is to compete for a female during mating season. Bucks bring their antlers together and push each other back and forth. The male that does the most pushing gets the chance to mate with the chosen female.

Leaving her fawns alone

The mating season of the white-tailed deer begins in September and lasts until February. In spring a pregnant **doe** makes her nest on the forest floor in a bed of dried leaves and grasses. One or two **fawns** are born sometime between April and June.

A mother deer licks her reddish brown fawns all over immediately after they are born. Unlike other animals she leaves her young alone most of the time during the first part of their lives. She returns to the nesting place several times a day to nurse her fawns but leaves after a short visit. She does this because she does not want to leave her scent as a trail for predators. The babies are safer left alone because they have very little scent when they are first born and are well camouflaged against the forest floor.

Browsing for food

Deer are herbivores and eat a great variety of plants. Instead of eating a large amount of food all at once, white-tails graze, moving from place to place, nibbling on food along the way. Because deer are very shy and nervous animals, they tend to do most of their feeding in the semi-darkness of dawn and dusk. They eat fresh, green leaves, the twigs of shrubs, the lower branches of trees, and many kinds of grasses. Their other favorite foods include fruit, seeds, acorns, and water lillies, as well as evergreen needles, and spruce or white pine branches in the winter.

A buck and doe white-tailed deer

The mule deer

Although the white-tailed deer is the most common deer in North America, the mule deer is better known to westerners. Mule deer live all along the west coast of the continent on the edges of coniferous mountain forests.

Telltale tails

Mule deer and white-tailed deer are similar animals, but there are some obvious differences between the two. Mule deer have larger ears and are stalkier. They have a "telltale tail" just as white-tailed deer do, but their tails are short and white with a black tip. When mule deer are frightened, they run away with their tails down. White-tailed deer speed away with their white tails held high in the air.

The main beam of antlers on each side of a mule deer's head branches into a "y," and each arm of the "y" forks again. A white-tailed deer's antlers do not divide in the same way. Look at this closeup of a white-tailed deer's antlers and compare it to the antlers of a mule deer buck on the opposite page.

A buck and doe mule deer

The elk

It is fall and the male elk's roar can be heard in the open wilderness. Why is he **bugling** so loudly? The louder and stronger a male's bugling is, the more females he will attract. He may then mate with these females. Noisy bulls also succeed in scaring away other bulls that may want to mate with the same females.

Harems and herds

Elk bulls mostly use their antlers to compete with one another during mating season. A bull with large antlers and a powerful neck is able to attract more females and defeat rival bulls. A strong bull may lead a **harem**, a group of ten or more cows, during the fall mating season. Most elks lose their antlers in the winter, but the ones that live in the open wilderness may keep them all year long for protection.

When the cold weather arrives, a bull leaves its harem and either joins a small group of male elks or spends the winter alone. The cows, young adults, and calves also come together to form a **herd**. In the spring cows prefer to bear their calves alone. In the summer the calves are brought into the herd. Harems are formed once again in autumn.

Fewer in number now

At one time in North America the elk was found all over the western plains. Over-hunting, starvation, and disease have greatly reduced their numbers. Now these animals are only found in the forested and mountainous areas of western Canada and United States.

Male elk have a spectacular set of antlers that can grow to a length of almost 2 meters and weigh almost 14 kilograms!

The black bear

Most black bears have long, coarse coats of black fur, but some black bears aren't black at all! They can be cinnamon colored or have a bluish tint to their fur. Some are even white! A fully grown black bear is about two meters long, with a short tail, long muzzle, and small, rounded ears. Its short, tightly curved claws allow it to scramble quickly up a tree.

A hearty appetite

Black bears are best described as **opportunistic omnivores**. They eat almost anything that is available. In late summer and fall they fill up on acorns and hazelnuts; in spring there are more than enough tender young plants to eat. Black bears also stuff themselves at berry-picking time. If there is a garbage dump nearby, they eat paper, rags, or even pieces of wood. If they are hungry for a little protein and come across a wasp or an ant nest, black bears scoop up a pawful of insects. Although they prefer to eat plants, they never turn their noses up at a dinner of fish, mice, rabbits, or young deer.

Winter beds

All this eating increases the store of fat that provides the bear with energy during its long winter rest. The bear often remains drowsy for several months. It makes its winter den in a cave, rock crevice, hollow log, or sometimes just in a mossy hollow under the low, sweeping branches of a spruce tree. When it has snowed heavily, the den sometimes becomes completely covered in snow except for a tiny breathing hole. You can spot a bear den by looking for a small puff of vapor that pops out of the hole whenever the bear breathes out.

The wolf

Many mammals prefer to spend their time alone, but wolves live in groups, called **packs**. A pack tends to have from four to seven members but may have as many as fourteen. It is usually made up of a single wolf family, including parents, pups, and other relatives.

Within each pack there is a leader who is the most important wolf in the pack. The leader is usually the father of the pups. The other males in the group are next in importance, followed by the mate of the leader, the other females and, finally, the pups from strongest to weakest.

The members of the wolf pack stay together when they hunt. They find their prey by tracking animal scents and by prowling. Wolves hunt deer, elk, and moose. If there are no large animals about, wolves eat small animals, such as mice and voles, or even insects.

Lone wolves

Not all wolves are pack members. Some travel alone. They are known as "lone wolves." Lone wolves are usually wolves that have lost their places as pack leaders to other stronger males. Sometimes lone wolves are young wolves that have left the pack to find a mate and start a pack of their own. A lone wolf is considered to be an enemy by other wolves and is often killed if it meets a pack.

All in the family

Wolf dens are usually located near water and can be found in almost any sheltered spot in the forest. Pups are born sometime in May. The average litter contains four to seven blind, floppy-eared, bluish grey pups.

Wolf families are closely knit. The whole pack helps in the education of the young. The members spend a great deal of time together playing games and training the pups. Playing games is important because it teaches the young how to live and hunt. When the pups grow up, they remain with the pack and take part in hunting and in caring for future pups.

Big, bad wolf?

Everyone has heard stories about the "big, bad wolf." The early settlers in North America were frightened by wolves because wolves hunt in packs and howl in an eerie way at night. These predators occasionally attacked the sheep and other animals that the settlers were raising for food.

There are many old stories about wolves attacking and eating people. There is, however, little proof that wolves are a great threat to people. A wolf will not harm a human being unless that wolf is starving, sick with rabies, or defending its life. Wolves do not howl to be frightening, either. They howl to mark the location of a pack's territory and to warn other wolves to stay away from it. Wolves may also howl just because they enjoy it!

Unfortunately, the mistaken ideas about wolves have caused much harm to these beautiful animals. For many years people were actually paid to kill them! Today very few wolves are left in the United States and in some parts of Canada.

A healthy herd

Wolves are an important part of the food chain in the forest ecosystem. They hunt and kill weak, old, or sick animals, leaving the strongest animals to carry on. A strong deer or elk can easily escape an attack. By killing off the weak, the old, the injured, and the diseased, wolves help keep a herd healthy. If only the healthy and strong members of the herd survive, they will be the ones that have babies, and their babies will also grow up healthy and strong.

The lynx

When you look at a lynx you can easily tell that it is a member of the cat family. Like other cats, it has hypnotizing eyes, sensitive whiskers, and a majestic presence. However, the lynx is about three times as big as the average house cat. Black markings sharply outline its ears. Wisps of black fur extend above the ears, forming pointed ear tufts. The tip of the lynx's rather short tail is also black. A striped ruff of fur dangles from its jaw.

The snow traveler

This forest cat lives in the northern woodlands. It is well adapted to life in a cold climate. A coat of thick, gray fur keeps it snuggly warm throughout the harsh winter. Its long legs and broad, hairy snowshoe feet allow it to prance across the surface of the snow with hardly a dent.

Silent and solitary

The lynx, like other cats, is a quiet and solitary creature. It rarely makes any noise, except for the loud calls of the male during mating season. The lynx spends most of its time hunting alone in its territory. It marks its territory off by leaving its scent on bushes and snowdrifts. When other lynx smell this scent, they know that they should stay away. When food is scarce, several lynx may hunt or live together, although each still marks off its own small territory.

Furry gray kittens

Female lynx make their dens in caves, hollow logs, or under rocky ledges. In early summer two or three kittens are born. The young look like little gray balls of fur with pale-colored stripes on their backs and limbs. For about three months the family stays together in the den and the father helps provide food for the kittens. By the fall the young lynx are ready to follow their mother as she teaches them how to catch their own food.

No hares for supper?

The lynx is a nocturnal animal. From two hours after sundown until dawn it prowls the forest looking for prey or lies under bushes ready to pounce. Its favorite food is the snowshoe hare. An adult lynx eats up to two hundred hares in a single year.

Unfortunately for the lynx there is not always a steady supply of hares to hunt. Every ten years there is a shortage. During these periods the lynx survives on other prey such as rodents, birds, and young deer. When hares are scarce, fewer female lynx have babies and fewer babies are born to each litter. If the hare shortage lasts a few years, the total lynx population drops. Many of the older lynx die off and there are not enough young lynx to replace them.

The skunk

There are four different kinds of skunks. All of them are black and white but each kind has a different set of stripes on its back. The skunk in the picture is the striped skunk. It has two stripes that run down the sides of its body to the end of its tail. It also has a big, white spot on the top of its head.

Living separately

Skunks live alone for most of the year. It is only during the mating period from late February until early March that males and females meet without fighting. After mating, the female nests in a warm, dry spot until the middle of May. At that time five or six young skunks, called **kits**, are born. The kits are blind, deaf, and wrinkled, but their black-and-white pattern is already outlined. By the time they are two months old, the kits are ready to go out on their own.

Nature's vacuum cleaner

A skunk will eat almost anything. Small animals such as mice, rats, snakes, frogs, and rabbits are part of its diet, but insects are a special favorite. The skunk does such a great job of finding and eating whole colonies of insects that it could be called nature's vacuum cleaner! Grasshoppers, grubs, beetles, and even bees are sucked up by a hungry skunk. A skunk is fussy, however, when it comes to eating caterpillars. It rolls their hair off so it doesn't have to eat the fuzz! During the summer a skunk also eats fruit, corn, garden crops, and the eggs of birds.

Winter rest

In the southern parts of North America skunks are active all year round, but in the north they den up for long periods in the wintertime. In October or November skunks make underground burrows or dig holes under buildings. They line their beds with grass and leaves. Skunks become sleepy from early December to late March. Sometimes several skunks den together to keep one another warm.

Skunked!

If you happen to meet a skunk while walking through the forest, the last thing you want to do is make threatening noises or actions. A frightened skunk might think that you are an enemy and decide to use its unique system of self-defense—its **musk glands**. These glands are located at the base of the skunk's tail and produce a yellowish, bad-smelling, eye-stinging liquid. Once you have been skunked, it is very difficult to smell sweet again!

Rodents

When we think of **rodents** we often think of rats and mice, but rodents come in many shapes and sizes and live in a variety of habitats. On the following pages you will meet four different forest rodents: the deer mouse, the eastern chipmunk, the porcupine, and the flying squirrel. All rodents have sharp, powerful front teeth that never stop growing. Rodents are constantly gnawing, so they don't ever have to worry about their teeth getting too long! Some rodents use their sharp teeth to dig underground burrows and even chop down trees.

The deer mouse

The deer mouse gets its name from the color of its fur. Its coat is reddish brown on top and white underneath, just like the coat of a deer. The deer mouse is one of the noisiest animals in the forest. It can often be heard squeaking, trilling, and chittering, but the most dramatic sound it makes is a shrill buzz. This buzz may last up to ten seconds and can be heard up to twenty meters away! Because it can hold this note so long, the deer mouse is sometimes called the "singing mouse."

Prey to many

This little rodent occupies a very important place in the food chain. It is eaten by almost every other living creature in the forest—from snakes to squirrels, fish to bears, weasels to owls—its predators are many.

The deer mouse hunts for its food during the night. It is omnivorous, so its diet includes many things. It eats various kinds of seeds, grains and fruits, all kinds of insects, and even animals that have been killed by other creatures.

Babies, babies, babies

Deer mice are capable of breeding all year long, although they rarely breed in winter. Most litters are born sometime between April and October. Anywhere from one to nine young mice are born in a single litter. A healthy female may give birth to ten or more litters within a year. Having so many babies keeps the deer mouse population constant even though many of these animals are eaten every day.

Back home again

Most deer mice make their nests on the ground, although a few settle up in trees. No matter what kind of home they make, they never lose track of where they live. They can even find their way home from a distance of several kilometers.

The eastern chipmunk

Chipmunks are alert, active little rodents that scamper around the forest all day long. They look somewhat like small squirrels, although their tails are flat instead of bushy. They have reddish brown fur and white bellies. All chipmunks can be identified by the alternating dark-and-light stripes that run down their backs from their shoulders to the bases of their tails. The chipmunk in the picture is called an eastern chipmunk because it only lives in the eastern regions of Canada and the United States. Its stripes are a little different from the chipmunks found farther west.

All they think about is food!

Chipmunks eat seeds, berries, nuts, and dried plants. They also like animal food such as slugs, worms, frogs, and salamanders. Although chipmunks spend most of their time gathering food, they do not eat all the food they find right away. They stuff some of it into stretchy pouches on the insides of their cheeks. They hide this extra food in underground burrows or in holes they dig close to where they have found the food. They can dig it up later when they are hungry. Because their food is scattered all over the place, chipmunks sometimes forget where some of it has been hidden. The seeds in the forgotten hiding places often grow into plants.

Always on the lookout

Chipmunks are prey to many animals, so they must constantly be on guard. When a chipmunk spots a predator, it runs up a tree to escape and says, "Chip, chip, chip!" to signal to the others that a dangerous intruder is nearby. It can make 130 "chip" sounds in one minute, even with its cheek pouches full of food.

Hidden burrows

Many chipmunks dig long burrows just below the earth's surface. Sometimes these burrows are up to ten meters long with many side chambers and escape hatches. Despite its size you might not be able to find a burrow even if you were standing right on top of it. This clever little rodent is careful to hide its home under a root or rock. When the chipmunk is digging its burrow, it carries away the earth in its cheek pouches. It scatters the dirt all around so there is no telltale heap near the entrance.

Resting underground

When winter comes, the chipmunk retires to its burrow and blocks off the entrance with dead leaves and dirt. It makes a bed at the end of one of the side passages, lining it with soft, warm materials such as rabbit fur, poplar or willow cotton, deer hair, shredded feathers, and parts of plants. It sleeps close to its hoard of winter food, which might contain two or more kilograms of seeds! It wakes up about every two weeks to snack on some seeds and to get rid of its body's waste products.

Spring fever

Sometime in April the males awake from their winter sleep. The females wake up soon after, just in time for breeding season. Near the end of May, litters of four to seven chipmunks are born in an underground burrow or in a comfortable heap of grass in a hollow tree.

The porcupine

How would you like it if your name meant "spiny pig?" You may not, but if you were a plump, pointy-nosed porcupine, you might not mind so much—especially if some of your hair had grown into extra-sharp **quills**.

Each porcupine has around thirty thousand brown-tipped quills covering its whole body except for its nose and belly. These quills are a great defense against the porcupine's enemies. Beneath the quills is a coat of soft, thick fur that keeps the porcupine toasty warm during the cold winter months. The quills are not noticeable when the animal is calm because they lie flat against its body and blend in with its fur. When the animal is frightened, it bristles out its quills and shakes its body. If a predator touches the porcupine, the quills stick into the intruder's skin.

A porky tree-climber

The porcupine lives in mixed forests but prefers hemlock and pine trees. It is well adapted to climbing trees even though it has a slow-moving, clumsy body. Its short and strong, knock-kneed legs help it climb as it digs its claws into the tree trunk. Even its tail gets involved in climbing. The tail supports the porcupine's body as the animal scrambles up and down the tree.

In the wintertime porcupines live in a den in a hollow tree or underground. They may even find and use an unoccupied cabin as their winter home. Several porcupines may den together to keep warm. In the springtime a single baby is born to a porcupine mother. At birth the baby is furry and its quills are soft, but they harden within a few hours!

Midnight snacks

The porcupine is a nocturnal animal. Although its eyesight is not very good, its senses of smell and hearing are excellent. It finds its favorite foods up in the trees. It eats twigs, bark, buds, and leaves. Because the porcupine is a rodent, it often gnaws on tough things in order to wear down its teeth. It especially loves salt, so it seeks out objects, such as ax handles and canoe paddles, that have been touched by sweaty human hands.

The flying squirrel

Have you ever been lucky enough to see a flying squirrel? Very few people have had this pleasure. Although the gray squirrel and the red squirrel are easy to see as they scamper through city parks and yards, the tiny flying squirrel is much more difficult to spot because it is only active at night. It spends its days curled up asleep in tree holes. If you did spot this night rodent, you would notice that it looks very much like its squirrel relatives, except that its body is smaller and its eyes are larger. Its large eyes help it see better in the dark. A flying squirrel's tail is shorter and looks flatter than other squirrels' tails because the fur is parted in the middle.

A furry hang-glider!

Despite its name the flying squirrel does not really fly. It does not have wings. There are two special flaps of skin along its sides that allow it to glide through the air from tree to tree. Together these two flaps form a furry membrane called a **patagium**. The patagium looks like a cape and stretches from wrist to ankle on both sides of the squirrel.

When the flying squirrel launches itself from a branch, it spreads its legs wide so that the patagium is stretched out and pulled tight. In this position its body acts as a hang-glider does. Sometimes this "flying" rodent glides for a distance of thirty meters before landing! It twists and turns while soaring through the air and changes direction by moving its tail and feet. These maneuvers allow it to land right on target. Being able to fly helps the flying squirrel dodge owls at night. Owls are its main predators.

This little squirrel can also bound along the ground or up and down trees at great speeds. To do this, it simply pulls the folds of its furry flap back and out of the way.

Daily nuts and seeds

Flying squirrels do not store large quantities of food as other squirrels do, so they look for food every night as they glide through the trees. They are omnivorous creatures. They have a mixed diet of nuts, seeds, blossoms, weeds, berries, grains, and insects.

Nesting together

In the summer the adult squirrels find nests in hollow trees high above the ground. They often take over abandoned woodpecker nests, lining them with bark, leaves, and moss. When winter comes, as many as twelve squirrels huddle together in a single nest to keep warm. By spring their home is more cramped than ever. An additional three to six bright pink, tiny, helpless babies share the nest with the adults. These little creatures are not helpless for long, though. By the time they are three months old, they have become expert gliders.

What's special about ...

the way a skunk sprays?

A skunk does not spray its **musk** unless its life is in danger. In fact, it gives a warning signal before it sprays. It lowers its head, growls, arches its back, and waves its tail. Then it stamps the ground with its paws. Some skunks stand up on their front feet to frighten away an intruder. If all these actions fail to scare the enemy, only then does the skunk fire its smelly musk. It can control its spray so it comes out as a wide mist or a long stream of fluid. A skunk can make a sure hit from three meters away.

If you happen to get sprayed, there are a few remedies for getting rid of the odor. Most people end up taking bath after bath until they are clean. Some people even throw away their sprayed clothes. You may have heard that bathing in tomato juice helps. It does. Given the choice, most people would rather smell like a tomato than a skunk!

a raccoon's hands?

A raccoon has extremely sensitive forepaws. When it is eating, it examines its food by touching and turning it. Sometimes a raccoon dips its paws into water while it is inspecting its food. It looks as if the animal is washing its food, but it isn't. It is actually making its forepaws more sensitive to touch by wetting them!

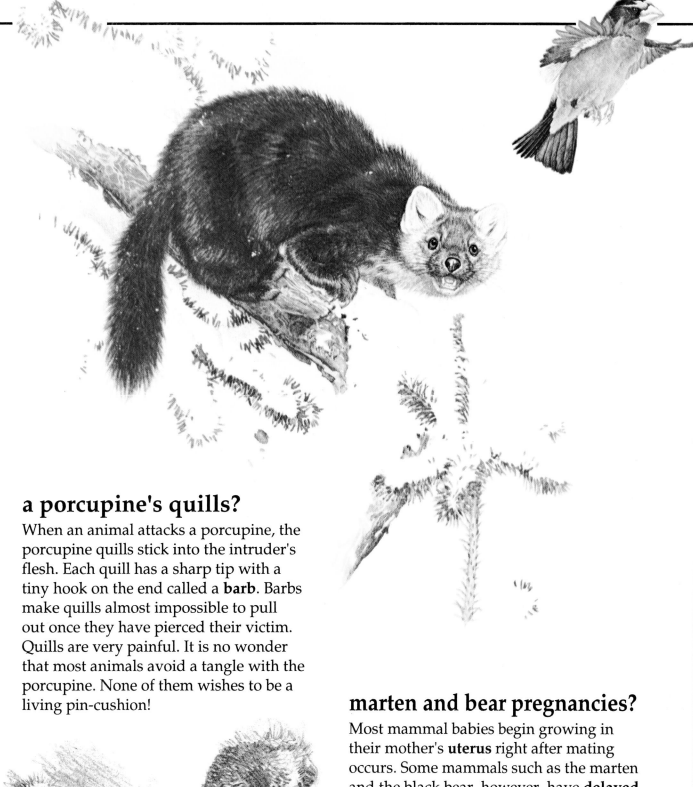

a porcupine's quills?

When an animal attacks a porcupine, the porcupine quills stick into the intruder's flesh. Each quill has a sharp tip with a tiny hook on the end called a **barb**. Barbs make quills almost impossible to pull out once they have pierced their victim. Quills are very painful. It is no wonder that most animals avoid a tangle with the porcupine. None of them wishes to be a living pin-cushion!

marten and bear pregnancies?

Most mammal babies begin growing in their mother's **uterus** right after mating occurs. Some mammals such as the marten and the black bear, however, have **delayed pregnancies**. After mating, their babies might not start growing for several months. The growth is delayed until the animal is healthy enough to give birth and raise babies. If the mother has not had enough to eat, the baby will never grow even if mating has taken place.

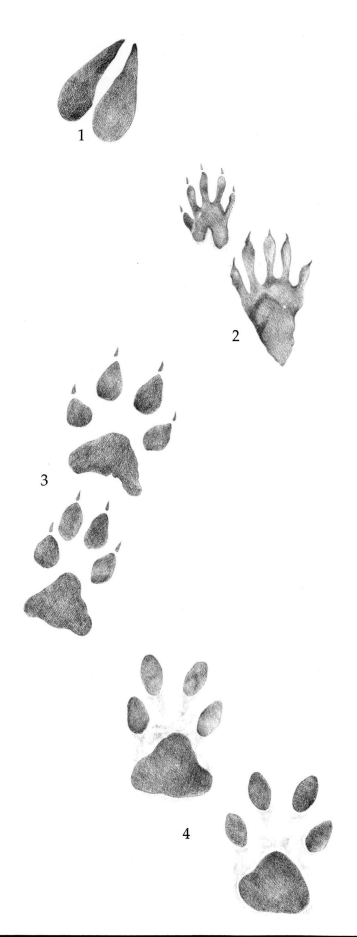

Activities

Where are all the animals?

Forest mammals are very difficult to spot because many of them are nocturnal. From dusk to dawn they are moving around and feeding. By day they are hidden in trees, thickets, holes, or other suitable resting places. Most mammals are shy of humans. They know when you are around and hide long before you have a chance to notice them. Their senses of sight, hearing, and smell are also much sharper than those of humans. You can, however, look for the telltale signs of animals. Next time you are walking in the woods, keep an eye open for burrow openings, fur caught on tree trunks, or tracks in the snow or mud. If you are patient and very quiet, you might be lucky enough to see a forest mammal.

To help you identify forest mammals, practise on the tracks found on these two pages. Which tracks belong to the following animals?

black bear	moose
chipmunk	porcupine
deer mouse	raccoon
flying squirrel	striped skunk
lynx	white-tailed deer
marten	wolf

(See page 56 for answers)

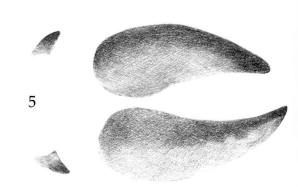

Putting garbage in its place

When people leave garbage in parks, yards, or by the sides of roads, they may be hurting animals and their young. Raccoons, squirrels, and sometimes even bears like people's garbage because they may find an easy meal. This habit, however, can be dangerous for animals. Wild animals sifting through trash are sometimes shot, run over by cars, or are injured by dangerous substances in the garbage. You can protect animals from harm by putting your garbage in a covered garbage can. Encourage your family and friends to do the same.

Helping wild animals

You can help wild animals by making a class donation to the World Wildlife Fund or another organization in your area concerned with conservation. The money your class raises can work to conserve wildlife in a number of ways. Your contribution might help biologists breed endangered birds in captivity for release into the wild. It may help pay for a biologist's trip into the wilderness to study animals or for some much-needed laboratory equipment. A small donation might even pay for the leg bands used in bird-tagging studies. Get in touch with a wildlife group or your local World Wildlife Fund office to see how you can help the wildlife in your area or country.

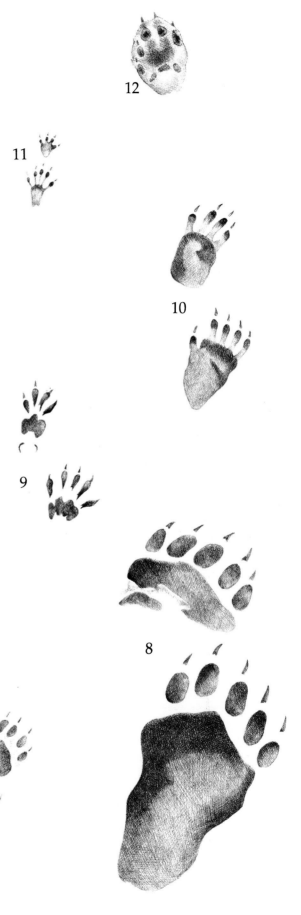

Illustrated by Elaine Macpherson

Dangers to forest mammals

In order to survive, all living creatures need food, shelter, and protection from danger. The forest environment provides all these things for the animals that live there. Unfortunately, many forests are no longer safe homes for their inhabitants. Forest fires, logging, and pollution are some of the dangers that are damaging or destroying wildlife.

Pollution

How would you like a smelly pile of trash in your living room? Many unlucky forest dwellers face just this situation. When people make certain products, the waste that is left over is often dangerous. Some of these waste materials are bottles, tires, oil, smoke, and chemical pollution from factories. Pollution not only damages forest plants, it harms all living things.

Logging

In many forests trees are cut down and used for wood and paper products. Sometimes new trees are not planted to replace the old ones that were cut down. The area is left alone to grow slowly back, or it is used for farmland or new buildings. The animals and plants that used to live in the forest cannot survive in the cleared area.

Forest fires

Sometimes forest fires start naturally, but most fires are caused by people. Campfires, burning garbage, and careless smoking are just some of the ways fires get started. When forests burn down, many plants and animals are destroyed. The animals that survive must find new places to live.

Lend a hand

We have mentioned just a few ways in which forest plants and animals are endangered. Can you think of some other dangers to forest wildlife? Find out how you and your class can take part in a program to conserve wildlife in a nearby forested area.

Glen Loates

Ever since Glen Loates was a child, his love of animals has led him to try capturing our natural world in drawings, paintings, and sculpture. As a boy he spent as much time as he could exploring neighborhood streams and woods. He started sketching interesting scenes during hikes and used these sketches to do more detailed illustrations.

Now, as a professional artist, Glen works in a light-filled studio in his own home. He has a natural history library and often borrows materials, such as animal pelts, from museums to help him make his paintings as realistic as possible. Glen also uses wildlife video tapes, clippings, and photographs from nature magazines as reference material for his work. Yet, no matter how much time Glen spends in the studio, he still thinks of the wilderness as his real working space.

A word from Glen

When I was a young boy just learning to draw, I was frustrated because I could not make my pictures realistic enough. Before long, though, I found out that I could greatly improve my sketches by doing them over and over. I took time to sketch every single day and, as if by by magic, my hands began to draw what my eyes were seeing.

If you are a budding nature artist, the best thing you can do is to draw as much as possible. Keep a daily sketchbook and hold onto both your good and bad drawings because they will help you see just how much your work has improved. If you start a collection of photographs and magazine clippings, you will have enough material with which you can practise sketching—but don't just work with other people's pictures. Take as many field trips as possible and create your own impressions of nature.

A surprised moose!

During his field trips, Glen has had many opportunities to observe and sketch wild animals up close—sometimes a little close for comfort! On one such journey, Glen and his brother came across a moose feeding in the water. They had just passed through a rough set of rapids in their canoe, when they floated within touching distance of a submerged moose. The startled moose raised his head, showing a huge pair of antlers covered with water lilies. The frightened animal quickly headed for shore while casting an angry glance back at Glen and his brother. Even though Glen was still shaken by the rapids, he managed to get a few sketches of the fleeing moose.

Glossary

antlers - Horns that branch out from the head of deer, elk, and moose. They are shed and replaced each year.

bugling - The act of making loud noises that resemble the sound of a bugle.

burrow - To dig a hole or tunnel.

community - A group of plants, animals, or people that live together in the same area.

coniferous (tree) - A tree that has cones.

consumer - A human being or animal that uses something made by someone or something else.

deciduous (tree) - A tree that loses its leaves.

ecosystem - The interacting community of plants and animals and the surroundings in which they live.

endangered - Very close to becoming extinct.

energy - The power needed to do something.

environment - The surroundings in which an animal or plant lives.

extinct - No longer alive or existing.

forepaw - An animal's front paw.

granary - A place that stores grain.

habitat - The area where a plant or animal lives.

harem - A group of females.

mammal - An animal that is warm-blooded, covered in hair, and has a backbone. A female mammal has mammary glands.

mammary glands - The organ in a female mammal that produces milk.

musk - The strong-smelling, oily substance that is produced by the musk glands of mammals such as skunks and martens.

muzzle - The front part of an animal's head that sticks out, including the nose, mouth, and jaw; a snout.

nocturnal - Active at night.

nutrient - A food substance that a living being needs to be healthy and strong.

omnivorous - Eating both plants and animals.

points - The ends of the branches of an antler.

pollution - Waste, such as chemicals and garbage, that harm ecosystems.

predator - An animal that eats other animals.

prey - An animal that is hunted and eaten by another animal.

producer - Someone or something that makes a product. A plant is a producer of food energy.

ravine - A narrow and deep valley that is worn away by running water.

rodent - A mammal that has large front teeth used for gnawing. Mice and squirrels are examples of rodents.

rut - The period of time when a male mammal, such as a moose, is ready to find a mate.

snout - A muzzle.

underbrush - Small plants, such as bushes and shrubs, that grow under large trees in a forest.

Answers to tracking activity on page 50

1. *white-tailed deer*
2. *raccoon*
3. *wolf*
4. *lynx*
5. *moose*
6. *chipmunk*
7. *striped skunk*
8. *black bear*
9. *flying squirrel*
10. *porcupine*
11. *deer mouse*
12. *marten*

Index

3456789 BP Printed in Canada 7654321098